W9-CFI-600

MONGOL EMPIRE

Virginia Loh-Hagan

45TH PARALLEL PRESS

Published in the United States of America by Cherry Lake Publishing Group
Ann Arbor, Michigan
www.cherrylakepublishing.com
Reading Adviser: Marla Conn, MS, Ed., Literacy specialist, Read-Ability, Inc.

Book Designer: Melinda Millward

Photo Credits: © CW Pix/Shutterstock.com, cover, 1, 28; © duncan1890/istockphoto.com, 4; © wynnter/istockphoto.com, 6; © Nastasic/istockphoto.com, 8; © rakushka13sell/istockphoto.com, 10; © ilbusca/istockphoto.com, 12; © Dmitry Chulov/Shutterstock.com, 14; © Sammy33/Shutterstock.com, back cover, 16; © ekipaj/Shutterstock.com, 18; © Fox3X/istockphoto.com, 20; © Ian Dyball / Dreamstime.com, 22; © oberto Castillo/Shutterstock.com, 24; © Gilad Fiskus/Dreamstime.com, 27

Graphic Element Credits: © Milos Djapovic/Shutterstock.com, back cover, front cover; © cajoer/Shutterstock.com, back cover, front cover, multiple interior pages; © GUSAK OLENA/Shutterstock.com, back cover, multiple interior pages; © Miloje/Shutterstock.com, front cover; © Rtstudio/Shutterstock.com, multiple interior pages; © Konstantin Nikiteev/Dreamstime.com, 29

Library of Congress Cataloging-in-Publication Data

Names: Loh-Hagan, Virginia, author.
Title: Mongol Empire / by Virginia Loh-Hagan.
Description: Ann Arbor : Cherry Lake Publishing, [2020] | Series: Surviving history | Includes index.
Identifiers: LCCN 2020003306 (print) | LCCN 2020003307 (ebook) | ISBN 9781534169098 (hardcover) | ISBN 9781534170773 (paperback) | ISBN 9781534172616 (pdf) | ISBN 9781534174450 (ebook)
Subjects: LCSH: Mongols—History—Juvenile literature.
Classification: LCC DS19 .L636 2020 (print) | LCC DS19 (ebook) | DDC 950/.2—dc23
LC record available at https://lccn.loc.gov/2020003306
LC ebook record available at https://lccn.loc.gov/2020003307

Printed in the United States of America
Corporate Graphics

TABLE OF CONTENTS

INTRODUCTION

The Mongol Empire grew to include what are now China, Pakistan, Persia, Iraq, and many more countries.

Genghis Khan was known as the founding father of the Mongol **Empire**. An empire is a group of nations ruled by a shared leader. The Mongol Empire formed in 1206. It was one of the world's largest empires. Today, the country of Mongolia is between Russia and China.

Khan was a great warrior. He was a powerful leader. He fought in many wars. He united the **tribes** in northern China. Tribes are groups of people. He organized **hordes**. Hordes are armies. Khan conquered more land than anybody in history. He killed between 30 million and 40 million people. He made a path through Asia and Europe. He connected East and West. He had great ideas. He paved the way for **modern** thinking. Modern means new and fresh.

After Genghis Khan's death, the Mongol Empire split into 4 parts: the Yuan Dynasty, Il-Khanate, Chagatai Khanate, and Golden Horde. Each part was ruled by its own khan.

The 13th and 14th centuries were known as the Age of Mongols. Mongols were **nomads**. Nomads are people who move from place to place. Mongols lived in the **steppes** of Central Asia. Steppes are dry, grassy plains. Mongols hunted. They gathered. They lived off the land.

Mongols introduced a writing system. They respected different religions. They created a postal system. They supported free trade. They built the Silk Road. They had a *Yassa* code. *Yassa* code was an honor code. It banned stealing. It banned cheating. It banned lying.

The Mongol Empire was ruled by the **khagan**. Khagan are rulers. Each Mongol ruler was called khan. The Mongol Empire was eventually defeated by the Chinese.

SURRENDER OR DIE?

Mongol hordes split their forces. They attacked from many directions at once.

Mongols spread terror. They spread panic. They raided. They invaded. They tortured. They took kingdoms by force. They allowed people to **surrender**. Surrender means to give in. Mongols protected those who submitted to their rule. If people resisted, Mongols destroyed them. They made sure people couldn't fight them in the future. They also wanted to send a message to others. They wanted to be feared.

Mongol hordes conquered hundreds of cities and villages. They killed millions of men, women, and children. They destroyed property. They tore down buildings. They burned farms. People **starved**. To starve is to die of hunger.

QUESTION 1

What would you have done if Mongol hordes were heading your way?

A You showed your skills. Mongols were known to spare engineers, **craftsmen**, and doctors. Craftsmen make things. Mongols found these people to be useful.

B You surrendered. You heard about the Mongols. You knew what they could do. You wanted to avoid war. Mongols treated surrendered people well. They made them part of the new Mongol Empire.

C You resisted. Mongols attacked. They fought until they won. They killed leaders.

Mongol soldiers talked to each other during battle. They used signals. They used flags. They used whistling arrows.

SURVIVOR BIOGRAPHY

Oghul Qaimish was married to Guyuk Khan. She gave birth to 2 sons. Her sons' names were Khoja and Naqu. When Guyuk Khan died, she became the leader. She wasn't a great leader. The French wanted to team up against the Muslims. Qaimish refused the French. She demanded submission. She also increased taxes for peasants. She required them to pay 1 animal for every 10 that they had. Before her, the tax was 1 in 100 animals. Qaimish held power until the year 1251. Then, Mongke Khan was elected ruler. Qaimish tried to kick him out. She lost. Mongke Khan took Qaimish prisoner. He put her on public trial. He accused her of **treason**. Treason is disloyalty. Qaimish was found guilty. She was wrapped in a sack. She was thrown into a river. This was the punishment for Mongol witches. Her sons were banished. Her grandson was killed.

HORSE OR NO HORSE?

Mongolian horses were small and strong.

Mongol warriors were **mounted archers**. Mounted means on a horse. Archers shoot bows and arrows. Mongols could shoot while riding horses. They could shoot while facing backward. They could shoot hanging from one side. They could shoot arrows over 1,000 feet (305 meters). They put armor on their horses. This way, their horses acted like shields.

Mongols were skilled horsemen. They used their horses as weapons. Each soldier had 3 or 4 horses. They changed horses often. This let them travel at high speeds. This way, they didn't tire out the horses.

Mongols lived off their animals. They drank horse milk. They used their leather for clothes. They used their poop for fire. They used their hair for rope.

QUESTION 2

What type of Mongol soldier would you have been?
This is based on how much money you would've had.

A You were rich. You could afford armor. Your horses had armor. You wore iron chains. You wore leather strips to protect your arms and legs.

B You were part of the working class. The Mongol Empire gave weapons to all soldiers. They gave files for sharpening arrows. They gave leather sacks to carry weapons. The sacks kept things dry. They could be used as floats to cross water.

C You were poor. You didn't have your own horse. You walked. You fought on foot. You didn't wear armor.

Soldiers who lost their weapons would be punished. They could be whipped. They could be kicked out.

SURVIVAL BY THE NUMBERS

- Mongols killed over 1 million in Nishapur, Iran.
- The Mongol conquest of China took 74 years. Over 30 million Chinese people died.
- Mongols killed about 50 percent of Hungary's population.
- Mongols reduced the world's population by about 10 percent.
- About 16 million people today may be related to Genghis Khan. About 1 in 200 men are his descendants.
- Genghis Khan was buried in secret. His soldiers rode 1,000 horses over his grave. This was so no one could find him.
- Kublai Khan attacked Japan. In 1281, a typhoon destroyed his fleet of 4,000 ships. A typhoon is a tropical storm.
- Kublai Khan built a communication system. There were 1,400 postal stations. The stations used 50,000 horses, 8,400 oxen, 6,700 mules, 4,000 carts, 6,000 boats, 200 dogs, and 1,150 sheep. Riders covered 250 miles (402 km) a day.

FEAST OR FAMINE?

Mongol horses were used to win many battles.

The spring in the year 1241 was warm. There was plenty of food. Then, winter came. The Danube River froze over. In 1242, Mongol hordes invaded Hungary. They crossed the frozen Danube River. They destroyed cities for 2 months. Then, they **retreated**. Retreat means to back away. Mongols had to get back to an area with food.

Spring came early. Snow and ice melted. This caused flooding. This created wetlands. The ground wasn't solid anymore. This made it hard for Mongol hordes to move around. Also, this wiped out crops. There wasn't much grass. This led to a **famine**. Famines are times when there isn't much food.

Without grass, Mongol horses couldn't eat. Without horses, Mongols couldn't live.

QUESTION 3

How would you have handled the risk of famine?

A You retreated. You did this to make sure there was plenty of grazing for the horses. Your horde had a lot of horses. You needed land.

B You waited. You didn't retreat. But you didn't invade. You thought things would improve.

C You invaded. You didn't want to quit. You wanted to add to the Mongol Empire. You planned to take food from villages.

The steppes in Central Asia faced periods of **droughts**. Droughts are periods of low rainfall.

SURVIVAL TIPS

Follow these tips to survive a cold winter:

- Keep warm. Protect your body. Dress in layers. Air gets trapped between layers. This trapped air holds in your body heat. Layers let you control your body heat.
- Protect your face. Keep toes and fingers warm. These are extreme points on your body. Cold will attack these areas first and stop blood flow.
- Stay dry. Avoid sweating. Water on your skin makes you colder.
- Stay in warm places. Don't travel unless you have to. Save your energy.
- Have warm food and drinks. Eat beans, grains, and vegetables. Stay hydrated.
- Avoid hypothermia. Hypothermia is when the body loses heat. It can lead to death.
- Avoid frostbite. Frostbite is when body parts freeze. It causes tissues to die.
- Use snow as shelter. Snow insulates. It traps heat.

MAN OR WOMAN?

All Mongols learned to ride horses. They learned
to shoot with bows and arrows.

Mongol women had more rights than other women of their time. They led businesses. They served as religious leaders. They could own property. They could be educated.

While men went off to fight, Mongol women were in charge. They set up camps. They set up **yurts**. Yurts are tents. Mongol women took care of animals. They took care of wagons. They took care of military gear. They cooked. They raised children.

Mongol men were fighters. But women were put in charge of hordes. Women and children were placed at the back of hordes. This made the hordes seem bigger than they were. Mongol hordes did this to scare their enemies.

QUESTION 4

Which role would you have played in the Mongol community?

A You were a woman or child. You helped as needed. You stayed at camps during battles. You took care of the horses. You prepared food for the fighters.

B You were a woman leader. You stepped up as needed. You followed behind the main hordes. You led much slower wagons of supplies and horses.

C You were a man. You served as a fighter. You were in battles. You were on the front line.

Mongol women made felt by pounding sheep's wool. They also made material from animal skins.

SURVIVAL TOOLS

Mongols' main weapon was the Mongol bow. These bows were recurve bows. They had limbs that curved away from the archer when released. They were more forceful than other bows. They had more speed. The core was made of wood. The horn was on the bow's belly. The belly was the side facing the archer. Animal muscle was on the back of the bow. Everything was bound together with animal glue. Mongol bows were powerful. They were efficient. They were small enough to be used on horseback. Mongol archers carried 2 to 3 bows. Heavy bows were used on the ground. Lighter bows were used on horseback. Mongols used bird tail feathers on the arrows. Tail feathers flowed more smoothly through the air. They rotated more accurately. They had good balance in the air. Mongols used metal arrowheads for war.

SICK OR HEALTHY?

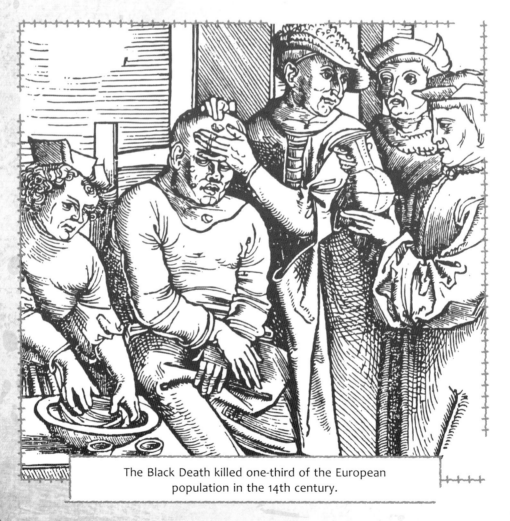

The Black Death killed one-third of the European population in the 14th century.

Plagues are sicknesses that spread. The bubonic plague was also called the Black Death. It was spread by fleas. Fleas picked up germs when they bit into infected animals or people. They passed on germs to others.

Mongol hordes may have spread the Black Death. Black Death appeared in Asia in the 1330s and 1340s. Mongol hordes used infected bodies as weapons. They flung dead bodies at their enemies. This made people sick.

Mongols traded. They raided. They had much contact with others. They traveled on horseback. This spread the Black Death.

Black Death killed over 25 million people in Asia. Over 300 Mongol tribes died. This may have led to the end of the Mongol Empire.

QUESTION 5

What would have been your risk of getting the Black Death?

A You didn't live in Asia or Europe. Black Death traveled on the Silk Road. It also traveled because of Mongol invasions.

B You stayed away from animals and people. You washed in hot water. You wore clean clothes. You stayed close to burning fires. You stayed in open areas. You used mint.

C You were a Mongol fighter. Mongols lived close together. They camped at battlegrounds.

A Mongol could ride for days after being infected.
Then, he or she would fall over and die.

SURVIVAL RESULTS

Mongols had spies. They collected information about their enemies.

Would you have survived?

Find out! Add up your answers to the chapter questions. Did you have more **A**s, **B**s, or **C**s?

- If you had more **A**s, then you're a survivor! Congrats!

- If you had more **B**s, then you're on the edge. With some luck, you might have just made it.

- If you had more **C**s, then you wouldn't have survived.

Are you happy with your results? Did you have a tie? Sometimes fate is already decided for us. Follow the link below to our webpage. Scroll until you find the series name *Surviving History*. Click download. Print out the template. Follow the directions to create your own paper die. Read the book again. Roll the die to find your new answers. Did your fate change?

https://cherrylakepublishing.com/teaching_guides

DIGGING DEEPER: DID YOU KNOW...?

The Mongol Empire was exciting. Mongols achieved great things. But many lives were lost as well. Surviving history involves many different factors. Dig deeper. Consider some of the facts below.

QUESTION 1:

What would you have done if Mongol hordes were heading your way?

- Mongol hordes were huge. They were noisy.
- Mongols launched surprise attacks. They did fake attacks.
- Mongols had a lot of practice with fighting.

QUESTION 2:

What type of Mongol soldier would you have been?

- Halberds are 2-handed poles. They were given to rich soldiers.
- All soldiers were given clubs, swords, axes, or spears.
- By age 3, Mongols learned to ride horses.

QUESTION 3:

How would you have handled the risk of famine?

- Some experts think Mongol hordes retreated because their khan had died. They needed to return to Mongolia. They needed to elect a new khan.
- Dzud is a Mongolian word. It means severe winter. It's when animals die due to starvation.
- Five separate Mongol hordes invaded Hungary.

QUESTION 4:

Which role would you have played in the Mongol community?

- Mongol children were tied to horses at first. This was part of their training.
- Men could have several wives. One wife was appointed senior wife.
- Men and women could do each other's jobs. This was for survival.

QUESTION 5:

What would have been your risk of getting the Black Death?

- Mongols attacked Caffa in 1346. Caffa refugees fled. They spread Black Death to Europe.
- Mint keeps away fleas.
- The Black Death would spread quickly in cramped places.

GLOSSARY

archers (AHR-churz) people who shoot with a bow and arrows
craftsmen (KRAFTS-men) skilled workers who can make things
droughts (DROUTS) periods of low rainfall
empire (EM-pire) group of nations ruled by one leader
famine (FAM-in) extreme lack of food
hordes (HORDZ) groups, armies
khagan (KAY-guhn) Mongol rulers who were individually called khan
modern (MAH-durn) new and fresh

mounted (MOUN-tid) on horseback
nomads (NOH-madz) people who move from place to place
plagues (PLAYGZ) sicknesses that spread easily
retreated (rih-TREET-tid) withdrew or backed away
starved (STAHRVD) died of hunger
steppes (STEPS) dry, grassy plains
surrender (suh-REN-dur) to give in
treason (TREE-zuhn) disloyalty
tribes (TRYBZ) groups of people
yurts (YERTS) circular tents used by Mongol nomads

LEARN MORE!

- Bjorklund, Ruth. *Mongolia*. New York, NY: Children's Press, 2017.
- Burgan, Michael. *Empire of the Mongols*. New York, NY: Chelsea House, 2009.
- Loh-Hagan, Virginia. *The Real Genghis Khan*. Ann Arbor, MI: Cherry Lake Publishing, 2019.

INDEX

ABOUT THE AUTHOR

Dr. Virginia Loh-Hagan is an author, university professor, and former classroom teacher. She wrote a 45th Parallel Press book about Genghis Khan. She lives in San Diego with her very tall husband and very naughty dogs. To learn more about her, visit www.virginialoh.com.